D1083727

READY, SET, RACE!

By Barbara Bazaldua

A Division of Insight Editions, LP
San Rafael, California

WELCOME TO
RADIATOR SPRINGS,

the cutest little town in Carburetor County and the place Lightning McQueen calls home. After a big smash-up on the Los Angeles International Speedway, Lightning returns to Radiator Springs to recuperate, but he wonders if his racing days are over. Knowing that Lightning feels discouraged, his Radiator Springs friends encourage him to believe in himself again. That's what good friends do.

HOW WELL DO YOU KNOW THE MOVIES?
How many streetlights are there in Radiator Springs?

(see back for answers)

95 LIGHTNING MCQUEEN

isn't just a world-champion racer. He is also a champion friend who knows the value of friendship, teamwork and teaching others. Lightning's racing career is second to none, but when the next-generation racers come on the scene, Lightning begins to wonder if he is still "faster than fast." As he faces a crossroads in his career, Lightning learns what racing really means to him. And it's not just about bringing home Piston Cups! *Ka-chow!*

STATS

- 2006 custom-built Piston Cup racer
- Full Race V-8 with 750 horsepower
- 0-60 in 4 seconds
- Top speed 198 miles per hour

"QUICKER THAN QUICK, FASTER THAN FAST. I AM SPEED!"
-LIGHTNING MCQUEEN

MACK

Whether it's to the Rust-eze Racing Center, Fireball Beach, Thunder Hollow Speedway, or wherever Lightning needs to go, Mack is ready to roll. The good-hearted, reliable race transporter has been with Lightning since the beginning of his career. Over time he has become Lightning's friend and confidant. When Lightning needs sound advice, Mack will always steer him right.

BEST BUDDIES

> "YOU KNOW ME,
> BUDDY. I'M ALWAYS
> HAPPY TO HELP.
> THINK I AM BETTER
> AT THAT THAN MOST
> FOLKS. YOU KNOW,
> TALKIN' AND STUFF."
> -MATER

MATER

Everyone could use a best friend like Mater. Underneath all that rust, the friendly, good-natured tow truck has a heart of pure gold. Cheerful, honest, and loyal, Mater always sees the bright side of things and the best in everyone. After Lightning's big crash, Mater hopes Lightning will continue racing. In fact, he gives his best buddy the idea of looking for the crew chief who taught Doc Hudson long ago. It's great advice!

BOOM CRANE WITH TOW CABLE AND HOOK ON BED

MISSING HOOD

ORIGINAL BLUE COLOR SHOWS THROUGH RUST

BIG SMILE

FUNNEST THINGS TO DO:
- Tipping tractors
- Driving backwards
- Flying in a helicopter
- Helping cars
- Going fishing for his hood
- Cheering on his best buddy

HOW WELL DO YOU KNOW THE MOVIE?
What does Mater say he's best in the world at doing?

HOW WELL DO YOU KNOW THE MOVIES?
Where did Sally live before moving to Radiator Springs?

"DON'T FEAR FAILURE. BE AFRAID OF NOT HAVING THE CHANCE. YOU HAVE THE CHANCE! DOC DIDN'T."
–SALLY

SALLY

Sally stays busy in Radiator Springs running the Cozy Cone and Wheel Well. But she always makes time to attend Lightning's races. Sally believes in Lightning, but she won't put up with him feeling sorry for himself after his crash. She tells him he has what it takes to keep racing and that it's time he stopped moping and started doing what he loves again.

51

DOC HUDSON

Although Doc Hudson, the Fabulous Hudson Hornet, is gone, his memory lingers on. Lightning knows exactly how much he owes Doc, who was his friend, mentor, and crew chief. Even though the two cars didn't hit it off at first, Doc and Lightning eventually became great friends. The Fabulous Hudson Hornet found new meaning in his life by becoming Lightning's crew chief and mentor. As Lightning questions his career in racing, he remembers and is inspired by his old friend's words of wisdom.

"THERE WAS A LOT LEFT IN ME I NEVER GOT A CHANCE TO SHOW 'EM."
-LIGHTNING REMEMBERING DOC'S WORDS

STATS

- Most wins in a single season

- Was known as the Fabulous Hudson Hornet

- Racing number was 51

- Taught Lightning how to race on a dirt track

- His racing contemporaries call him "Hud"

INSPIRING FRIENDS

GUIDO

At every race, the determined and talented Guido changes Lightning's tires faster than you can say "pit stop." Guido's high-energy enthusiasm is infectious. It always makes Lightning smile!

HOW WELL DO YOU KNOW THE MOVIES?
How many Piston Cups did Doc Hudson win?

 LUIGI

As enthusiastic as ever, Luigi travels with Lightning to his races, making sure he has a plentiful supply of Lightyear tires. Lightning is inspired by Luigi's loyal support.

RACETRACK PALS

Lightning McQueen has enjoyed a long and legendary racing career, and he has the Piston Cups to prove it. He's also made a lot of great new racing friends. They may be rivals on the track, but they are always the first to congratulate each other. They love to hang out and share a laugh or two. These racers all share the belief that the love of racing is more important than winning and that good sportsmanship and friendship are more valuable than trophies.

HOW WELL DO YOU KNOW THE MOVIES?
How many Piston Cups has Lightning McQueen won thus far in his career?

BOBBY SWIFT #19

Fun-loving Bobby likes to spar with Lightning on the track, and they are often wheel-to-wheel as they race to the finish line. Sometimes he even manages to squeeze past Lightning at the last second to win the race. Although Bobby is a racing rival, Lightning enjoys his sense of fun and fair play, so it's a shock to him when Bobby leaves the track behind for good.

CAL WEATHERS #42

Easy-going, good-natured Cal is Lightning's competitor on the track, but off track, the two pals are always ready to congratulate each other and share a laugh. Cal has an impressive winning record and a great attitude, but the new generation of racers is making it harder for him to stay ahead, so Cal decides it's time to hang up his racing tires for good.

BRICK YARDLEY #24

If there's one thing Brick loves more than racing, it's the friendships he has made during his racing career. He and Lightning have competed on the track for years, but that hasn't stopped them from being great friends. Lightning is upset when he learns that Brick has been replaced by a next generation racer.

NEXT GENERATION RACERS

To Lightning's dismay, the racing world is changing. Newer, faster cars equipped with more technology are competing, and Lightning is having a harder time beating them. Although Lightning is a little worried, he's determined to meet this new challenge and prove he still has what it takes to rule the track.

20 JACKSON STORM

Winning has always been easy for Jackson Storm, a cocky Piston Cup rookie. But the overconfident young racer lacks practical experience—and wisdom—on the track. He also lacks courtesy. It's not enough for this brash, rude racer to win. He likes to put down other race cars—especially Lightning—every chance he gets.

"GOOD LUCK OUT THERE, CHAMP! YOU'RE GONNA NEED IT!"
-JACKSON STORM

STATS

- 2017 Custom-built 'Next-Gen' Piston Cup Racer
- Maximum Performance V-8 with 850 hp
- 0-60 in 3.6 seconds
- Top Speed of 214 miles per hour

NEXT GENS
GEARING UP TO GO

CHASE RACELOTT
- Second generation Piston Cup racer
- Has top technology and track smarts
- Knows what it takes to win

DANNY SWERVEZ
- Newcomer to racing
- Fast, focused learner
- Pushes himself to the limit

RYAN "INSIDE" LANEY
- Third generation Piston Cup racer
- Talented and charming
- A favorite with fans

BUBBA WHEELHOUSE
- Next Generation stock car racer
- Drives and lives fast and furious
- As a champion for diversity, he believes every race car deserves a lane on the track.

HOW WELL DO YOU KNOW THE MOVIES?
What does Jackson Storm use to train?

TRAINING TIME

Following a big smash-up during a race, Lightning is fully repaired but needs to get back in shape, so he heads to the new Rust-eze Racing Center for training. With its up-to-date technology, Lightning is sure the center will help him get up to speed again.

"I HAVE BEEN A FAN OF YOURS FOREVER. AND NOW TO BE YOUR SPONSOR? HOW GREAT IS THAT?"
-STERLING

STERLING

Smart, dashing Sterling, the new owner of Rust-eze, runs one of the largest racing centers in the country. Although Sterling is friendly, relaxed, and casual, he always has his headlights focused on what's best for his business. He wants to be sure his investment in Lightning McQueen and the number 95 pay off big—whatever it takes. Sterling makes a deal with Lightning. If Lightning wins, he can continue racing. But if he loses, he must retire and focus on selling the 95 brand.

CRUZ RAMIREZ

Cruz Ramirez is a top-notch trainer at the Rust-eze Racing Center, and her unusual training methods have helped a lot of rookies make it to the big time. She's so good that her boss, Sterling, calls her the "Maestro of Motivation." But Cruz once dreamt of racing, too. Training Lightning reawakens those dreams, and eventually she gets the chance to prove if she has what it takes to be a star on the track.

"I'VE WANTED TO BE A RACER FOREVER! BECAUSE OF YOU!"
-CRUZ RAMIREZ

STATS

- 2017 CRS Sports Coupe
- High Performance DOHC V-6
- 0-60 in 3.8 seconds
- Top Speed of 210 miles per hour in race trim

TRAINING TIME

Fed up with Cruz's off-beat training methods, Lightning insists he's ready for the racing simulator. He's not. He smashes into virtual walls, vehicles, a drinking fountain, and then crashes for real. It's a virtual training disaster.

When Lightning decides to train on Fireball Beach, Cruz accompanies him. Unfortunately, she doesn't know how to drive on sand, so Lightning ends up coaching her. He spends more time training his trainer than on working out himself.

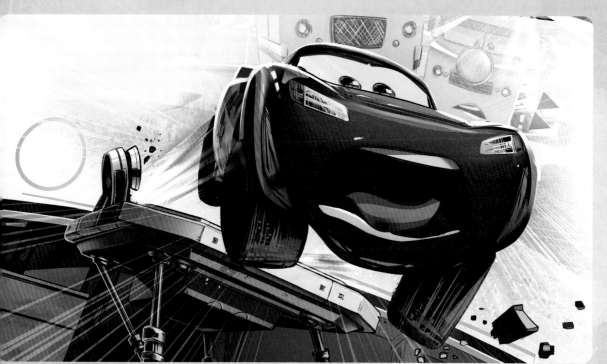

HOW WELL DO YOU KNOW THE MOVIES?
How many times does Lightning hit the virtual wall while on the simulator?

TRAINING LIST:
-Fuel up with good breakfast
-Dance class
-Slow laps on treadmill
-Nap
-Name tires and get to know them

DOWN 'N' DIRTY CRAZY EIGHT

Disappointed in his racing times at Fireball Beach, Lightning heads to Thunder Hollow Speedway, where he thinks he can practice on a dirt track with real racers. It's a dirt track, all right, but he arrives on "Family Night," when the featured race is the Thunder Hollow Crazy Eight demolition derby. Lightning and Cruz are caught in the middle of the action with no way to escape. They have to do some very fast desperate and down-and-dirty driving. Although Cruz only plans on tracking Lightning's speed from the infield, she's soon a target herself and is forced to join the competition. Lightning helps Cruz dart, dodge, and swerve to safety. In fact, she even wins a trophy!

ARVY
R.V. CAMPER WITH 'TUDE
BEST MOVE:
PLAYING ROUGH
LOVES: SMASHING ANY-
THING WITH WHEELS

MISS FRITTER
SCHOOL BUS
KNOWN AS: THE DIVA
OF DEMOLITION
LOVES: TEACHING OTHER
CARS WHO'S BOSS

"LOOKIE HERE BOYS! WE GOT US A COUPLE OF ROOKIES!"
-MISS FRITTER

HOW WELL DO YOU KNOW THE MOVIES?
What number does the pitty spray on Cruz before the demolition derby begins?

DR. DAMAGE
EMERGENCY VEHICLE
BEST MOVE: SPEEDY TURNS
LOVES: CRUSHING THE COMPETITION

TACO
SHAPED LIKE A TACO FROM BEING HIT TOO MANY TIMES.
BEST MOVE: SQUEEZING BETWEEN CARS
LOVES: HIS TACO-INSPIRED PAINT JOB

LESSONS FROM THE "LEGENDS"

The big race at the Florida International Super Speedway is fast approaching, and Lightning feels more and more desperate. He's spending too much time watching after Cruz and not enough time training. To make matters worse, Sterling tells Lightning if he doesn't win the Florida 500 race, he should retire. Lightning has to win that race and prove Sterling wrong!

    Then good-old Mater says something that gets Lightning thinking. The only car smarter than Doc was the car who trained him! That's it! Lightning decides to find Smokey, Doc's old crew chief, and ask for help. To his delight, once Lightning reaches Thomasville Speedway, Doc's home track, he finds not just Smokey but a lineup of legendary racers who knew and respected Doc and are ready to help Lightning rev up his training and ramp up his mojo.

"YOU'LL NEVER BE AS FAST AS STORM. BUT YOU CAN BE SMARTER THAN HIM."
-SMOKEY TO LIGHTNING

SMOKEY

A great mechanic and crew chief, Smokey helped put "The Fabulous Hudson Hornet" on track for greatness. Crafty and tough, Smokey may be gruff and opinionated, but he always wants to do right by his friends—and that includes Lightning.

RIVER SCOTT
Scrappy early Piston Cup racer

LOUISE "BARNSTORMER" NASH
The fearless "First Lady of Racing"

JUNIOR "MIDNIGHT" MOON
Souped up jalopy famed for
back road racing

SWEET TEA—NASH'S
FORMER PITTY
Now a country singer

TRAINING TIME

According to Smokey, Lightning needs to work on his driving strategy.
He needs to trust his instincts and start using his smarts more than just his speed.
With Cruz geared up as Lightning's sparring partner, the two begin to train together.

TRAINING LIST:
- Pull oversized trailer up hills
- Dodge flying hay bales
- Weave through stampeding tractors
- Drive without lights at night

THE RACE IS ON

At last, Lightning and Cruz arrive at the Florida International Super Speedway. The stakes are high. Lightning's friends and fans believe in him, but others are sure he doesn't stand a chance. With Sterling's deal still in place, Lightning has to win if he hopes to continue racing. It seems as if everything Lightning cares about is hanging on this race.

LADIES AND GENTLECARS . . .
START YOUR ENGINES

1. Lightning gets off to a great start, races hard, and quickly moves from last place to the mid-twentieth spot.

2. Lightning overhears Sterling telling Cruz to get back to the training center where she belongs. At that moment Lightning realizes something: Cruz IS a racer—and deserves a chance to show what she can do.

3. A few cars crash on the track, meaning all racers must head to their pits. Lightning screeches into the pit and tells his pit crew to get Cruz race-ready. Geared up and wearing his number—95—Cruz is going to finish the race for Lightning! He is giving her a shot at making her dream come true.

4. As Cruz roars onto the track, Lightning stands near Smokey on the crew chief podium. Lightning tells Smokey what to say to Cruz, using all the training experiences they've shared. Eventually, Lightning takes over for Smokey on the crew chief stand. Cruz draws closer and closer to Storm, and as he tries smashing her into a wall, she remembers what Smokey told her about a move Doc once used in one of his races. She does an amazing flip over Storm, just like Doc, and crosses the finish line first. She's the winner!

5. Cruz has found her new place in the racing world. So has Lightning. He has a lot of racing left in him, but for now he's going to be like Doc and mentor a talented new racing star. And he's going to have a blast doing it!

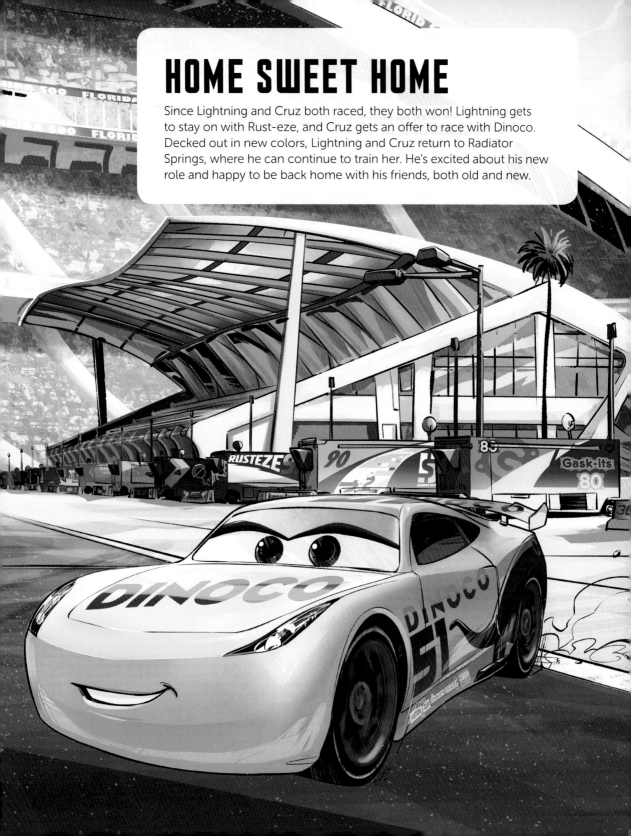

HOME SWEET HOME

Since Lightning and Cruz both raced, they both won! Lightning gets to stay on with Rust-eze, and Cruz gets an offer to race with Dinoco. Decked out in new colors, Lightning and Cruz return to Radiator Springs, where he can continue to train her. He's excited about his new role and happy to be back home with his friends, both old and new.

MAKE IT YOUR OWN

Create the true king of the racetrack as you decorate your Lightning McQueen model. Before you start building and decorating, choose a theme and make a plan. Anything goes! Read through these sample projects to get you started.

LIGHTNING MCQUEEN

WHAT YOU NEED:
- *Paintbrush*
- *Fine paintbrush*
- *Paints (light red, red, dark red, yellow, orange, blue, white, black, gray, and silver)*

WHAT YOU MIGHT WANT:
- *Silver metallic pen*

IT'S BEST TO PAINT THIS MODEL AFTER IT HAS BEEN BUILT. PAY ATTENTION TO EACH PROJECT, THOUGH, AS THERE ARE SOME SPECIAL INSTRUCTIONS.

1. Paint the car body, spoiler, axles, and hubcaps red.

2. Paint the front window and the model's mouth white.

3. Paint the side windows gray and outline them in black.

4. Paint the tires black, and then, with a small detail brush, paint the word "Lightyear" on the tires in white.

5. For the Rust-eze signs, paint the interiors red-orange. Then use yellow to add the details and lettering.

6. Paint the "95" on the sides of the car yellow. Add red at the bottom, and orange in the middle. Dip your brush in water, and use the brush to blend the colors together slightly.

7. Paint a white outline around the "95." Then add a black outline.

8. Paint the lightning bolt behind the "95" and the flames above the back tires light yellow. Make sure not to paint the flames on the sides of the car just yet.

9. Outline the lightning bolt with a thin line of orange. Outline the orange with white, and then the white with black.

10. Paint the flames around the lightning bolt dark red.

11. With a silver metallic pen or silver paint, add the bolts on the car hood and the side mufflers in front of the back tires.

12. Paint the shape of the headlights and taillights in gray and add details—black, white, and orange paint to create the details for the headlights and orange, red, and white for the taillights.

13. For the eyes, paint the pupils black and the irises blue, with a highlight in white.

14. Add a small, gray lightning bolt on the front fenders and outline in black.

15. If you want, add the decals on the sides in blue and white or black and yellow.

16. Finally, add some light red to the inside of the mouth for Lightning McQueen's tongue.

ADIATOR SPRINGS CLASSIC

Radiator Springs is the cutest little town in Carburetor County and home to the some of the best paint jobs around. Lightning McQueen himself took on a whole new look during his first stay in Radiator Springs.

For this project, you can build Lightning McQueen with the back of the sides, roof, and hood facing outward, or so that the "95" and "Rust-eze" designs are hidden. You'll also want to leave off the spoiler. You'll need to add the oval shape yourself. Try sketching it out with a pencil and then filling it in with paint.

HE PISTON CUP CHAMPION

Lightning McQueen knows his way around any racetrack, but his heart has always been set on the Piston Cup. Now, you can use your model to unleash Lightning McQueen's inner champion with this stellar Piston Cup design.

For this idea, you can follow a lot of the steps from the first project, but you'll paint the base of the car gold instead of red.

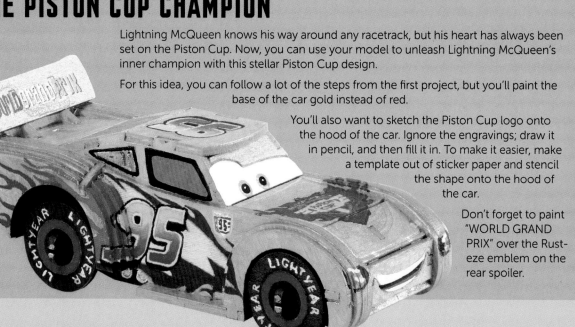

You'll also want to sketch the Piston Cup logo onto the hood of the car. Ignore the engravings; draw it in pencil, and then fill it in. To make it easier, make a template out of sticker paper and stencil the shape onto the hood of the car.

Don't forget to paint "WORLD GRAND PRIX" over the Rust-eze emblem on the rear spoiler.

INCREDI BUILDS™

IncrediBuilds™
A Division of Insight Editions, LP
PO Box 3088
San Rafael, CA 94912
www.insighteditions.com
www.incredibuilds.com

Find us on Facebook: www.facebook.com/InsightEditions
Follow us on Twitter: @insighteditions

Disney/Pixar elements © Disney/Pixar; rights in underlying vehicles are the property of the following third parties, as applicable:
AMC, El Camino, Gremlin, Hudson, Hudson Hornet, Nash Ambassador, Pacer, Plymouth Superbird and Willys are trademarks of FCA
US LLC; Dodge®,Jeep® and the Jeep® grille design are registered trademarks of FCA US LLC; FIAT is a trademark of FCA Group
Marketing S.p.A.; Fairlane and Mercury are trademarks of Ford Motor Company; Chevrolet, Chevrolet Impala, and Monte Carlo are
trademarks of General Motors; Mack is a trademark of Mack Trucks, Inc.; PETERBILT and PACCAR trademarks licensed by PACCAR
Inc, Bellevue, Washington, U.S.A.; Petty marks used by permission of Petty Marketing LLC; Carrera and Porsche are trademarks
of Porsche; Volkswagen trademarks, design patents and copyrights are used with the approval of the owner Volkswagen AG;
Background inspired by the Cadillac Ranch by Ant Farm (Lord, Michels and Marquez) © 1974.

Published by Insight Editions, San Rafael, California, in 2017.
No part of this book may be reproduced in any form without
written permission from the publisher. All rights reserved.

Library of Congress Cataloging-in-Publication Data available.

ISBN: 978-1-68298-122-1

Publisher: Raoul Goff
Associate Publisher, Children's Division: Jon Goodspeed
Acquisitions Manager: Robbie Schmidt
Art Director: Chrissy Kwasnik
Designer: Leah Bloise
Project Editor: Rebekah Piatte
Production Editor: Lauren LePera
Editorial Assistant: Erum Khan
Associate Production Manager: Sam Taylor
Model Design: Liang Tujian, Team Green

ROOTS of PEACE   REPLANTED PAPER

Insight Editions, in association with Roots of Peace, will plant two trees for each tree used in the
manufacturing of this book. Roots of Peace is an internationally renowned humanitarian organiza-
tion dedicated to eradicating land mines worldwide and converting war-torn lands into productive
farms and wildlife habitats. Roots of Peace will plant two million fruit and nut trees in Afghanistan
and provide farmers there with the skills and support necessary for sustainable land use.

Manufactured in China by Insight Editions

10 9 8 7 6 5 4 3 2 1

TRIVIA ANSWERS:

Page 4: 1
Page 8: Driving backwards super fast!
Page 9: Los Angeles
Page 11: 3
Page 12: 7
Page 15: A high-tech Simulator
Page 19: 5
Page 21: 20